T.

Coffee Self-Talk™ Starter Pages

A Quick Daily Workbook to Jumpstart Your Coffee Self-Talk

Kristen Helmstetter

Green
Butterfly
Press

The Coffee Self-Talk™ Starter Pages

Copyright © 2022 by Kristen Helmstetter

ISBN: 978-1-958625-00-2

For information on excerpting, reprinting or licensing portions of this book, please write to info@greenbutterflypress.com.

V1.2

About the Author

In 2018, Kristen Helmstetter sold everything to travel the world with her husband and daughter. She currently splits her time between Arizona and a medieval hilltop town in Umbria, Italy. She writes romance novels under the pen name Brisa Starr.

Listen to *Coffee Self-Talk with Kristen Helmstetter* wherever you listen to podcasts.

You can also find her on Instagram: Instagram.com/coffeeselftalk

Other Books by Kristen Helmstetter

Coffee Self-Talk: 5 Minutes a Day to Start Living Your Magical Life

The Coffee Self-Talk Daily Reader #1 & #2: Bite-Sized Nuggets of Magic to Add to Your Morning Routine

Tea Time Self-Talk: A Little Afternoon Bliss for Living Your Magical Life

Pillow Self-Talk: 5 Minutes Before Bed to Start Living the Life of Your Dreams

Wine Self-Talk: 15 Minutes to Relax & Tap Into Your Inner Genius

The Coffee Self-Talk Guided Journal: Writing Prompts & Inspiration for Living Your Magical Life

Coffee Self-Talk for Teen Girls: 5 Minutes a Day for Confidence, Achievement & Lifelong Happiness

Coffee Self-Talk for Dudes: 5 Minutes a Day to Start Living Your Legendary Life

Introduction

Hello!

I'm so happy to continue your Coffee Self-Talk journey here with you, with *The Coffee Self-Talk Starter Pages*.

I expect that you've either already read the book, *Coffee Self-Talk*, or that you are reading it alongside this book. The purpose of these "starter pages" is to make your daily self-talk ritual as easy as possible and to help you get your magical life rolling faster.

This book uses a simple "fill in the blank" format, to help inspire your thinking when you write your own Coffee Self-Talk scripts. Go through this process once a day, for 21 days, and by the end, it is very likely to have become a long-term, regular daily habit.

By doing Coffee Self-Talk and the simple exercises in this book, you'll train your brain to think more positively, see goodness and opportunities around you, and manifest your magical life.

As you raise your baseline of happiness, you'll find that you start doing more things that support that happiness and well-being. Simply by showing up every day to do your Coffee Self-Talk, after a few weeks, you'll start to genuinely become a happier and more resilient person. And you'll find even more ways to make yourself happy, in a wonderful feedback loop.

It all starts with the ritual. The ritual becomes a habit, and the habit changes your life.

So let's get crackin' with some transformation!

Love,

How to Use This Book

This book has 21 days of starter pages. Each day has six pages to go through while you drink your cup of coffee. Each day should only take you about 10 minutes or less.

The format for each day is as follows:

Page 1   Inspiring content that will motivate you and get you excited for the day.

Page 2   Pre-made affirmations. Try to speak these out loud, if possible.

Page 3   The "I Am" activity. Simply fill in the blanks with things that you love about yourself or would like to become. These become your own, short, punchy affirmations. Once you've filled in the blanks, read them aloud, if possible. Repeat as many times as you'd like. It's also perfectly fine to repeat the same affirmations from one day to the next. In fact, repetition is very powerful. But it can also be fun to mix things up.

Here are some examples:

- I am loved.

- I am amazing!

- I am creative.

- I am wealthy.

- I am generous.

- I am ready to rock!

Page 4 A short, fill-in-the-blank gratitude exercise.

Page 5 Here is where you write your own Coffee Self-Talk. I detail how to do this in Chapter 5 of the main book, *Coffee Self-Talk*, so refer to those pages if you need a refresher.

There are 8 blank lines, and you can write your self-talk as one affirmation per line. You can repeat the I AM affirmations if you like, you can write new affirmations, or you can lift from the scripts I provide in Part 2 of the main *Coffee Self-Talk* book. Or a mix of all three. It's totally up to you.

You can make the self-talk particular to that day, or it could be looking into the future, designing your long-term destiny.

Page 6   The "One Goal" page. This is where you write down one goal you're going to accomplish on that day. Why one goal? Because sometimes we overwhelm ourselves with so many things to get done, that we hardly get anything done! By listing just one goal, you focus your efforts, and you're much more likely to accomplish it.

Your goal for the day should be something small, realistically doable in one day. For extra credit, make it a goal that supports your affirmations, or takes a step toward your long-term, dream-life destiny.

And that's it!

This book is designed to be easy, quick, and fun to get your Coffee Self-Talk ritual going. And when you finish the 21 days, you might like the format so much that you want to go through it all over again. If so, just get another book, or grab any blank journal or notebook and copy the process.

Let's begin!

Day 1

Today is the first day for setting your life up for smashin' success. You're here! Bravo! Woohoo! You showed up. Look at you, now! (You're awesome.) Seriously, do you realize how amazing and unique you are for doing this? You're taking charge of your life. You're taking responsibility. You're making a difference for yourself. That's huge! Pat yourself on the back because magical living is here.

Think it, feel it, and believe it.

Your belief in this process is one of the juiciest ingredients for the recipe of your destiny. Victory is inside you. You are transforming. You are incredible.

Today is my day.

Today, I have an abundance of time,
and energy, and love to start living my
magical life.

I am learning and growing. I am
transforming, becoming a new person.

I am full of possibilities,
and opportunities surround me.

Today, I claim the start of my
new, magical life.

Date ....

I am ready for my new life!

I am ....

I am ....

I am ....

I am ....

I am ....

I am passionate about my new life!

I am grateful for

....

I am happy because

....

....

I love ....

I love ....

I love ....

I love myself because I

....

....

Today's Coffee Self-Talk

One goal I will accomplish today

....

....

*"The universe conspires to reveal the truth
and to make your path easy
if you have the courage to follow the signs."*

—Lisa Unger

Day 2

You're NOW creating an empowering structure with each morning of your day. This gives you a feeling of control. It offers you a feeling of destiny. And this influences everything else!

You alone possess the qualities you need to be successful. Today, and every day you start like this, you'll find yourself smiling more, attracting better things, trying new things, and overall just being in a good mood. Now doesn't that sound amazing?

My thoughts are filled with
positivity, energy, and love.

Prosperity is all around me. I am in the right
place at the right time,
and I set myself up for success.

If there are challenges, I reach into my mind
for the best mindset. I overcome and learn,
and I get stronger as a result.

The more I learn, the better prepared I am
for anything that comes my way.

Mistakes are treasured lessons. I am infinite.
My life is amazing.

Date ....

I am excited for my day!

I am ....

I am ....

I am ....

I am ....

I am ....

I am excited for my life!

I am grateful for

I am happy because

I love

I love

I love

I love myself because I

Today's Coffee Self-Talk

One goal I will accomplish today

....

....

"I like things to happen.
And if they don't happen,
I like to make them happen."

—Winston Churchill

Day 3

Humor elevates your emotions... it feeeels great, and it heals.

Look for the funny in life all day today. There is comedy everywhere in life, books, on the internet, or TV. Actively seek it. Attract it. Be it!

Laugh at silly mistakes, spills, and trips. Laugh at circumstances, no matter what they are. Trust in the laughs to come.

I'll get you started...

Did you hear about the French cheese factory that blew up?

There was nothing left but de Brie.

I am funny. I laugh. I am jolly.

I am full of mirth. I am giggles and smiles.

I love humor. Comedy fills my cup.
Funny things find me all day.

Laughter is love. And I love laughter.

He he he. Ha ha ha. Ho ho ho. La la la.

Giggle giggle, snort snort. Life is funny!

My life is filled with silly and funny
experiences.

Date ....

I am ready for laughter today!

I am ....

I am ....

I am ....

I am ....

I am ....

I am laughing every day!

I am grateful for

I am happy because

I love

I love

I love

I love myself because I

Today's Coffee Self-Talk

One goal I will accomplish today

....

....

"A good laugh is sunshine in a house."

—William Makepeace Thackeray

Day 4

Putting in the work...

Manifesting your dream life isn't about sitting on a couch and expecting your desires to come true. It's about taking action. *Working at it.*

Want more love in your relationships? *You must give* more love. Want better health? *You* start... by changing your thinking and your self-talk, then making smarter choices.

You want more money? First, get your brain in the game with self-talk... think it, and feel it. Believe in the power and magic of your mind, learn something new, and see all the opportunities around you when you change your focus. *And then take action!*

My future is up to me. I am in charge.

I start with my thoughts and words
I choose to let dance in my head.

I get excited about those words, and they
start to stir emotions in my heart.

I am worthy.

I keep these feelings at the forefront of
my day, and it opens my eyes to see new
opportunities on my horizon.

I know I'm on the right track.

I am me. I am love. I am successful.

Date ....

I am ready to take action!

I am ....

I am ....

I am ....

I am ....

I am ....

I am passionate about my goals!

I am grateful for

....

I am happy because

....

....

I love ....

I love ....

I love ....

I love myself because I

....

....

Today's Coffee Self-Talk

One goal I will accomplish today

....

....

*"People are just as happy as they
make up their minds to be."*

— Abraham Lincoln

Day 5

Your Coffee Self-Talk affirmations will increase your confidence because you're training your brain with new words, thoughts, and beliefs.

With repetition (saying your self-talk every day), you'll find yourself gaining in confidence more and more. You'll be in a better mood, happier, and smiling more. Things that used to upset you won't nearly as much.

That's the magic of all of this! If you used to hesitate, don't be surprised if you find yourself jumping in and loving it. You will program yourself to be more confident, and you'll no longer even be consciously thinking about it.

Go, you!

I am confident and transforming,
right here and right now.

I'm training my brain for success by simply
showing up to my life with the right words,
thoughts, and feelings.

I am in a great mood, and it feels so good!

I am worthy of success. You are worthy of
success. We are all worthy of success.

The whole universe conspires to
help me manifest my best life.

I am ready.

Date ....

I am confident about my day!

I am ....

I am ....

I am ....

I am ....

I am ....

I am confident about my life!

I am grateful for

I am happy because

I love

I love

I love

I love myself because I

Today's Coffee Self-Talk

One goal I will accomplish today

....

....

"I think, therefore I am."

—René Descartes

Day 6

Think the words, and feeeeel the feelings! That's the trick!

When I imagine the home I want, or a new skill, or the confidence to give speeches to large groups, I picture it in my mind. I see myself being successful, and I ask myself, "How would it *feel* to have that home, or that skill, or that confidence?"

It always feels good in my mind, because they are things I want. So, naturally, they feel good to imagine. Soak in those juicy feelings! Feel the sparkle and the glow. Relish this deliciousness. Then, take it with you into your day. You can tap into these images you're creating anytime, and the more often you do it, the better! Believe in you! Believe in your dreams!

I create my own life, and it starts with
the pictures I create in my head.

I am in charge of my imagination. When
I have vibrant, playful, and successful
images about myself and my life, it creates
a stronger belief in me, and this makes my
dreams come true.

This gives me energy to attract my great life.
This gives me the vibration I need to radiate
to manifest everything I desire.

It starts with me and ends with me.
It is always only me.

I am in charge.

Date ....

I am ready to manifest my dreams!

I am ....

I am ....

I am ....

I am ....

I am ....

I am full of love for my life!

I am grateful for

....

I am happy because

....

....

I love ....

I love ....

I love ....

I love myself because I

....

....

Today's Coffee Self-Talk

One goal I will accomplish today

....

....

"Action follows conviction, not knowledge."

—Pierre Lecomte du Noüy

Day 7

Hi. How are you feeling today? Are you feeling wide awake and excited to do another day of Coffee Self-Talk? Or are you perhaps feeling a little mopey and tired?

It doesn't matter, because everything is all good. Once you get going and change the dialogue in your mind to one of positivity and opportunities, gold and glitter, energy and verve, you will feel an uptick in your mood. Sometimes you go from zero to hero in an instant, and sometimes it's from a level three to a level four. It doesn't matter how big the improvement... any improvement is *awesome!*

Just keep showing up. Keep doing the work. You're drawing your dreams to you *right now*, as you read this!

I have beautiful energy. I tip my face to the sun and smile. I know that magic is happening behind the scenes for me.

When I direct my thoughts, it directs my focus, and this changes my behaviors. It changes my day, and my outcomes.

I attract people and things, based on my vibe and what my mind pays attention to.

The game of life is so simple: I am in charge of whether I'm happy or not. Having a great life or not. It's not circumstances. Oh no. It's about seeing the wonderful side to everything. What an incredible way to live!

Date ....

I am in charge of my life!

I am ....

I am ....

I am ....

I am ....

I am ....

I am attracting great things!

I am grateful for

I am happy because

I love

I love

I love

I love myself because I

Today's Coffee Self-Talk

One goal I will accomplish today

....

....

"He can fit his sails to every wind."

—John Clarke

Day 8

We usually think of self-talk as positive, but it comes in many flavors, from lousy to wonderful.

Whether positive or negative, any words you use to describe yourself and the world dictate the direction of your life. Do you criticize yourself? Do you criticize others? Or people on TV or social media? It's all self-talk, so be careful... your thoughts are a reflection of YOU!

Your self-talk determines what you attract, see, and do. You want great thoughts as often as possible to give you the greatest life. It's that simple. Love yourself as you are now. Love others. Wish the world happiness, no matter what. This all serves to make you feel better, and it puts out a better energy to help you make your dreams come true.

I look at my life and see the shine. I look around, and I notice the happy.

I surround myself with positive things, like upbeat music, playful people, beautiful nature, and things that inspire.

My thoughts become real.
I want a wonderful life,
so I think wonderful thoughts.

I'm on a blazing new adventure. It's empowering. It's exciting. My chest expands with awe, love, and gratitude.

Thank you, me. Thank you, brain.
Thank you, life.

Date ....

I am the master of my feelings.

I am ....

I am ....

I am ....

I am ....

I am ....

I am more than enough.

I am grateful for

I am happy because

I love

I love

I love

I love myself because I

Today's Coffee Self-Talk

One goal I will accomplish today

....

....

*"The only person you are destined to become
is the person you decide to be."*

—Ralph Waldo Emerson

Day 9

Repetition is the name of the game.

I've been doing Coffee Self-Talk for years, and I still show up every single day to do it. In fact, I do it throughout the day.

Self-talk has given me the most crazy-amazing life I ever could've imagined. And it will do that for you, too, when you show up every day.

Repetition is so powerful, you can never have too much. If you repeat one of your affirmations, such as *I am happy*, over and over, you will quickly notice a difference. It keeps you focused. It guides your feelings and drives your life. Repetition is *awesome*! Whatever thing you want more of, repeat thoughts and words about that thing!

I am happy.
I am worthy.
I am love.

I am happy.
I am worthy.
I am love.

I am happy.
I am worthy.
I am love.

I am happy.
I am worthy.
I am love.

Date ....

I am ready for my day of love!

I am ....

I am ....

I am ....

I am ....

I am ....

I am passionate about my life of love!

I am grateful for

....

I am happy because

....

....

I love ....

I love ....

I love ....

I love myself because I

....

....

Today's Coffee Self-Talk

One goal I will accomplish today

....

....

"We are what we repeatedly do.
Excellence, then, is not an act but a habit."

—Aristotle

Day 10

Your thoughts are energy. You know this because, when you start saying things like, "I love my life, I feel amazing, I am kind," you immediately start to feel better.

But if you say things like, "Life is hard, I have bad luck, I can't do anything right," your shoulders slump, and you feel dejected. There is no joy there. Ever.

But you are in control of your thoughts! They are a choice!

I wake up happy most of the time, but that doesn't mean I don't have occasional *OOOF* days. And on those days, I rely on my self-talk to lift me up. And soon, I feel better. I attract better feelings and experiences, just because I started the day with my positive words and thoughts.

I love being in control of my life
by using my mind.
It's like having special powers.
It's fun, like a fantasy.

I know the power of my brain. I know the
magic of my subconscious. I am always in
charge of how I respond to anything in life.

I choose whether I laugh and see the good
in anything, no matter what it is.
There's always something I can find.

Maybe it's gratitude, maybe it's love.
Maybe it's compassion.
But there's always something
good to be found.

Date ....

I am ready to control my mindset.

I am ....

I am ....

I am ....

I am ....

I am ....

I am having an excellent morning!

I am grateful for

I am happy because

I love

I love

I love

I love myself because I

Today's Coffee Self-Talk

One goal I will accomplish today

....

....

"You're much stronger than you think you are."

—Superman

Day 11

You are meant to live a wonderful life, and it starts with you. You are worthy of living an amazing life. You are worthy of love. Happiness. Peace.

You are destined to have an impact on the world.

When I have a great attitude, my energy changes. My family notices. My friends notice. My energy affects their energy. Then, they go out into the world with their elevated energy, and it spreads even more.

You have the power to effect change in the world. You can start a chain reaction. It starts with you, every day.

I impact other people simply by
focusing on my happy self.

When I become an example,
I bring about change.

When I smile, other people smile.
When I laugh in the face of circumstances,
other people witness this.

When they see me succeeding and attracting
abundance, and magic, and love, they want
the same for themselves.

I don't have to try to change others.
I simply change myself,
and they witness what is possible.

Date ....

I am ready to focus on me!

I am ....

I am ....

I am ....

I am ....

I am ....

I am passionate about my focus!

I am grateful for

I am happy because

I love

I love

I love

I love myself because I

Today's Coffee Self-Talk

One goal I will accomplish today

....

....

"Think globally, but act locally."

—René Dubos

Day 12

Do you know what the main difference is between a dull, ho hum life and one that's magical and glittery?

It's your self-talk! Your words and thoughts. That's the difference! Start your day with lightness and brightness by thinking and saying great things. Compliment yourself. Smile at your bed, your toothbrush, and the coffee pot. Feel grateful for your shoes, your home, your car. When you start with success words in your mind, you set up your whole day for success.

Blow yourself a kiss in the bathroom mirror! Yes, do this, *no matter how silly it feels!*

I love the new me!

I rise every morning with a glow,
I glide through the day on a breeze,
and I fall asleep with peace.

The colors of my skies light me up.
I am amazing. I am love. I am safe.

I pass a mirror and see my smiling
reflection, and I say, "Hey there, cutie!"

I'm alive. I'm alive. *I'm alive!*

I feel a new sunrise inside me,
radiating out in all directions,
filling the world with warmth and love.

Date ....

I am ready for everything!

I am ....

I am ....

I am ....

I am ....

I am ....

I am radiating passion for my life!

I am grateful for

I am happy because

I love

I love

I love

I love myself because I

Today's Coffee Self-Talk

One goal I will accomplish today

....

....

*"Whether you think you can
or you think you can't, you're right."*

—Henry Ford

Day 13

It's check-in time.

How have you been this past week? How are you right now? I ask because the energy and emotion you're feeling at this very moment is directing your life.

Do you feel tense or anxious? Are you stressed out? Change that right now. Think about puppies, or chocolate, or snuggling your cat. That's all it takes to switch your mindset.

Get your brain on track, and trust in the process. Start thinking, right now, of all the things you want in life. YOU are in charge, and it starts with your thoughts. You are worthy of your desires, but you need to take responsibility to make the magic happen! Ready! Set! *Go!*

I believe in me! I can do whatever I put my amazing, smart, beautiful mind to.

My epic life awaits! I am yanking up all the old gnarly weeds, and I'm planting sparkling, new rainbow seeds.

I hug myself, and hearts and stars wrap around me, soothing and strong, and full of belief. I can really do it. I *am* doing it!

I elevate myself and my magnificence. I am worthy of a wonderful life. It is safe to follow my truth, my love, my creativity, and my inspirations. My heart is safe. I am calm. I breathe in peace, and I exhale peace.

Date ....

I am ready to believe in me!

I am ....

I am ....

I am ....

I am ....

I am ....

I am worthy of living a wonderful life!

I am grateful for

I am happy because

I love

I love

I love

I love myself because I

Today's Coffee Self-Talk

One goal I will accomplish today

....

....

*"If you make your internal life a priority,
then everything else you need on the outside
will be given to you, and it will be
extremely clear what the next step is."*

— Gabrielle Bernstein

Day 14

The next time you bump into someone grumpy, find compassion in yourself, and wish them happiness. Wish for them to find joy and love. Reach into your pocket, grab a fistful of pixie dust, and blow it to them. It could be your boss, someone in the grocery store, or the leader of another country.

Wishing love and happiness is always the best move, because love is always the answer, no matter what. I mean, if grumpy people were happy, then they wouldn't be grumpy anymore, right? Mean people would cease to be mean.

Plus? Doing this makes *you* feel good! Sending love to someone else, and wishing them happiness, will always come back to you. Try it, and see!

I wish the world happiness today.

I wish for everybody to feel empowered
with love and kindness.

I wish generosity. And it starts with me... I
start with my own happiness. I empower my
life with love and kindness.

I am generous with others. We are all one.
We are all connected in some form.
When I give kindness, it comes back
to me like a boomerang.

When I give love, it comes back to me.
This is an amazing way to live.

Date ....

I am ready to have an amazing day!

I am ....

I am ....

I am ....

I am ....

I am ....

I am sending good vibes everywhere!

I am grateful for

I am happy because

I love

I love

I love

I love myself because I

Today's Coffee Self-Talk

One goal I will accomplish today

....

....

"Spread love everywhere you go."

—Mother Teresa

Day 15

Psst... hey, it's me, Kristen. I was just wondering... do you have any huge, wild, crazy, epic, dreams? Is there anything you feel a pulling in your soul that you want to do? Is there something that would be awesome to do but you wonder, "How would I ever do that?"

If you have a big idea, start writing about it in your self-talk. Trust me, crazy things can happen. I became a novelist when I didn't think I had a creative bone in my body. All I did was sprinkle some affirmations about it in my Coffee Self-Talk, repeated them every day for a few months, and then... *bam!*... I started writing romance novels! So if you have a dream, write it down. Repeat your beautiful, empowering self-talk every day. See yourself doing it. Believe in the possibility. And watch yourself go!

I have dreams, and I have the power
to make them become reality.

I use my words and feelings
to guide my life and attain my goals.
I can do anything I want.

I am strong, and smart, and capable.

I have the resources I need,
and if I need to learn something new,
I know that I can master it.

I am worthy of my dreams.
I attract the right things into my life.
I approve of myself one million percent!

Date ....

I am ready to manifest my dreams!

I am ....

I am ....

I am ....

I am ....

I am ....

I am passionate about my goals!

I am grateful for

I am happy because

I love

I love

I love

I love myself because I

Today's Coffee Self-Talk

One goal I will accomplish today

....

....

"Those who dare to fail miserably can achieve greatly."

— John F. Kennedy

Day 16

My journey into happiness and magical living was like peeling an onion. Every time I reached a new level and made my life better, I found something new to transform. Another layer to peel.

It was like I started with the big things first, but once those were taken care of, I found more little things to learn and change. But it turns out, these little things were full of juicy bits. They were little nuggets of magic.

The adventure you're on is life-long, and just when you think it can't get any better, it does! But you have to show up every day, do the work, and be intentional. Make the changes. Believe in the best, see the bright side, give love and thanks. These things fuel your magic carpet ride.

I show up to my life every day.

I show up and love myself.
I love myself relentlessly.

I show up to my day, for me, excited with
confidence about the adventure that awaits.

I am abundant and generous.
Prosperity is all around me.
Each day brings amazing new surprises.

I'm wide awake now.
I'm alert with self-love. I'm juicy, curious,
and I see possibilities everywhere.
The magic is all around me!

Date ....

I am feeling love and gratitude.

I am ....

I am ....

I am ....

I am ....

I am ....

I am happy and grateful!

I am grateful for

I am happy because

I love

I love

I love

I love myself because I

Today's Coffee Self-Talk

One goal I will accomplish today

....

....

"I am happy because I'm grateful. I choose to be grateful. That gratitude allows me to be happy."

— Will Arnett

Day 17

You're embarking on a new adventure in life.

You're driving in new directions. Think about your next "destination," whether that's a change in career, improved health, a new relationship, or more money. Are there things you could learn, or skills you could improve, or places you can hang out to help make your dream a reality?

Do you need new qualities or strengths? If so, how can you go about making some changes? Maybe it's eating better. Or joining a club. Or networking. Or just getting more sleep!

When you think about the big changes you want to make in your life, focus on the small, daily changes that will help make it happen.

I feel young and vibrant,
because I'm full of life
and rainbow energy.

I pop out of bed, I glide as I walk,
I dance through the day.
I have energy to be ME! *Finally!*

I slice through the mundane
to find the marvelous.

Ideas run through my veins.
My mind is bursting with good thoughts,
and I look around my space with awe.

Wow. I am so lucky to be alive.

Date ....

I am ready because I feel great!

I am ....

I am ....

I am ....

I am ....

I am ....

I am loving my body, mind, and soul.

I am grateful for

I am happy because

I love

I love

I love

I love myself because I

Today's Coffee Self-Talk

One goal I will accomplish today

....

....

"When we change,
everything else appears to change."

— Henri Amiel

Day 18

If you find yourself surrounded by people who aren't riding the same *awesome* magic carpet ride, no problem, just keep on going!

Keep your smile wide. You keep your sparkly eyes gazing toward the starry sky.

We lead by example. In time, those around you will either support you, join you, or fall by the wayside. Some will take time to come around. I've seen it happen!

Just keep working on you and your energy. That's all you need to do. What happens will happen, and you will find yourself on exciting adventures, meeting new people, growing, and transforming. Get ready for the most amazing ride!

I see the good.

I find the treasure.
No matter where I am,
I have this superpower.

When it's gray and cloudy,
I toss on my rose-colored shades.
I dig, dig, and dig until I find
something good about any situation.

It's my specialty.

I discover the light,
and it feels good.

Date ....

I am ready to see the good.

I am ....

I am ....

I am ....

I am ....

I am ....

I am passionate about the great!

I am grateful for

_____

I am happy because

_____

_____

I love _____

I love _____

I love _____

I love myself because I

_____

_____

Today's Coffee Self-Talk

One goal I will accomplish today

....

....

"The people who are crazy enough to think they can change the world are the ones who do."

— Steve Jobs

108

Day 19

Once you make up your mind to do something, or to make a change, then everything in your world changes, too. Things seem to magically appear to help you. It's as though the universe is conspiring to help you. In a way, that's what happens. But what really happens is that your eyes are now open to opportunities—which were always there, but now you can see them!

You'll also start putting out an amazing vibe, which translates into a bright energy that draws people and things to you like a butterfly to a beautiful flower.

Get ready for amazing synchronicities and experiences to find you!

I have made up my mind
to live my most spectacular life.

I have made up my mind
to choose good thoughts as often as
possible, like all the time!

I have chosen to think about the best,
knowing that the best is always available.

I know that choosing my words means
choosing the kind of life I want.

I want epic, so I think epic. I want happy, so
I think happy. I want love, so I think love. I
want peace, so I think peace.

Date ....

I am ready for fun synchronicities!

I am ....

I am ....

I am ....

I am ....

I am ....

I am full of magic!

I am grateful for

....

I am happy because

....

....

I love ....

I love ....

I love ....

I love myself because I

....

....

Today's Coffee Self-Talk

One goal I will accomplish today

....

....

"Once you make the decision, you will find all the people, resources, and ideas you need... every time."

— Bob Proctor

Day 20

Pretend! Make believe!

If you're struggling to change something about yourself, then just pretend. Make believe, like you're an actor playing a role in a movie. Imagine it, and act *as if*. Your brain doesn't know the difference!

For example, suppose you wish for a better relationship with someone, like your co-workers or mother-in-law. Simply *pretend* you have the best time together, and imagine that experience in your mind. It feels so much better!

Keep doing it, and just watch what happens. Just keep on pretending. Feel the fun! In time, you won't be pretending anymore, and the change will have become real.

I love my imagination,
and I'm so grateful to have one.

I can fill my mind with anything I want.
Castles, beaches, mountains.
Chocolate chips, flowers, and magic.
Happy people, overcoming
challenges, finding love.

My imagination is my power.
My imagination is where it all begins.

I envision my future. I love what I see.
It makes me feel amazing.

Thank you, imagination, thank you!

Date ....

I am ready to use my imagination!

I am ....

I am ....

I am ....

I am ....

I am ....

I am passionate about my imagination!

KRISTEN HELMSTETTER

I am grateful for

I am happy because

I love

I love

I love

I love myself because I

118

Today's Coffee Self-Talk

One goal I will accomplish today

....

....

"The greatest discovery you'll ever make
is the potential of your mind."

— Jose Silva

Day 21

Relax and surrender.

That's what you do once you've read, felt, and believed your Coffee Self-Talk. After that, turn your palms to the sky, and take a deep breath. You won't always know the "how" of manifesting something, but that's ok. That's the adventure!

Yes, sometimes it can seem frustrating, but then you go back to believing, and it makes you feel better! By saying your self-talk, thinking it, and feeling it, *and then letting it go*, you give your subconscious time to bake all your delicious ideas, desires, and dreams. A plan will emerge, and it's often something you never could've imagined. You'll look back someday, with a grin on your face, and say, "Wow, I never would've guessed it would happen this way."

I know the power of surrender.
It's a key part of manifesting.

I have peace of mind. I enjoy relaxing,
kicking my feet up, and letting my
subconscious do what it does best:
figuring things out for me!

It's awesome. It's brilliant.
Thank you, subconscious. Thank you for
always listening to my words
and helping me figure out the next steps.

I have total peace of mind.
My job is to be calm and patient, and then
open my eyes to all the doors of
opportunity that open in front of me.

Date ....

I am full of peace and patience.

I am ....

I am ....

I am ....

I am ....

I am ....

I am passionate about living in peace.

I am grateful for

....

I am happy because

....

....

I love ....

I love ....

I love ....

I love myself because I

....

....

Today's Coffee Self-Talk

One goal I will accomplish today

....

....

*"Life is like a box of chocolates.
You never know what you're going to get."*

— Forrest Gump

Conclusion & Free PDF

By doing your Coffee Self-Talk, you're setting goals. You're self-talking about things you want and changes you want to make in your life. These are all goals.

And our brains LOVE goals. They feel really good. And every step you take toward one of your goals feels super good, too. Every time you show up to your life to do your self-talk, it's like taking a step in the right direction.

Embrace it, love it, squeeze it, and play with it. As you continue your self-talk, you'll be inspired for new directions to take and new things to do. Enjoy the journey, smell the roses, and be excited about the magical life you're creating!

Free PDF

I'd love to hear from you! Email me at the address below to tell me how things are going, and what goals you're working on.

If you'd like to receive a FREE PDF preview from the forthcoming *Coffee Self-Talk Manifesting Playbook*, write to me, and be sure to ask for the "Manifesting Playbook PDF":

Kristen@KristenHelmstetter.com

You can also find me at:

- Instagram.com/coffeeselftalk

- Facebook.com/groups/coffeeselftalk

- *The Coffee Self-Talk Podcast with Kristen Helmstetter* — find it wherever you listen to podcasts.

And finally, I have a HUGE favor to ask of you.

If you would help me, I'd greatly appreciate it. If you enjoyed this book, I'd love it if you would leave a review for *The Coffee Self-Talk Starter Pages* on Amazon (even if you bought it somewhere else). Reviews are incredibly important for authors, and I'm extremely grateful if you would write one!

What's Next?

Here are a few more members of the Coffee Self-Talk family:

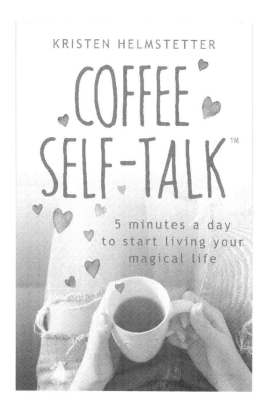

International Bestseller – Over 150,000 Copies Sold

Coffee Self-Talk:
5 Minutes a Day to Start Living Your Magical Life

Coffee Self-Talk is a powerful, life-changing routine that takes only 5 minutes a day. Coffee Self-Talk transforms your life by boosting your self-esteem, filling you with happiness, and helping you attract the magical life you dream of living. All this, with your next cup of coffee.

The Coffee Self-Talk Daily Reader #1:
Bite-Sized Nuggets of Magic
to Add to Your Morning Routine

This companion book offers short, daily reads for tips and inspiration. It does not replace your daily Coffee Self-Talk routine. Rather, it's meant to be used each day *after* you do your Coffee Self-Talk.

KRISTEN HELMSTETTER

TEA TIME SELF-TALK

a little afternoon bliss
for living your magical life

by the bestselling author of
COFFEE SELF-TALK

Tea Time Self-Talk:
A Little Afternoon Bliss
for Living Your Magical Life

The perfect 5-minute, afternoon break companion, designed to give you a blissful moment to yourself for reflection and motivation.

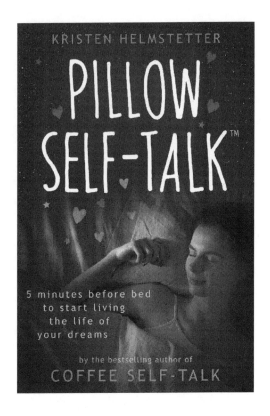

Pillow Self-Talk:
5 Minutes Before Bed to Start Living
the Life of Your Dreams

End your day with a powerful nighttime ritual to help you manifest your dreams, reach your goals, find peace, relaxation, and happiness... all while getting the *best sleep ever!*

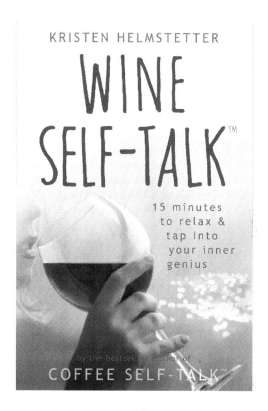

Wine Self-Talk:
15 Minutes to Relax & Tap Into Your Inner Genius

There is a source of sacred wisdom in you. Wine Self-Talk is a simple, delicious ritual to help you relax, unwind, and tap into your inner genius.

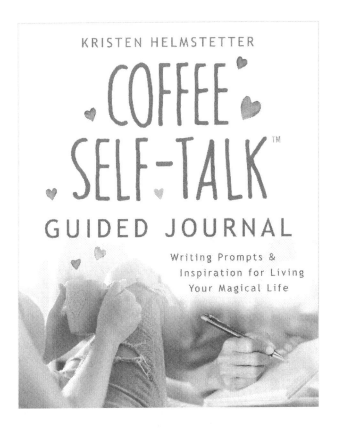

The Coffee Self-Talk Guided Journal:
Writing Prompts & Inspiration for Living Your Magical Life

This guided journal keeps you lit up and glowing as you go deeper into your magical Coffee Self-Talk journey. Experience the joy of journaling, mixed with fun exercises, and discover hidden gems about yourself. Get inspired, slash your anxiety, and unleash your amazing, badass self.

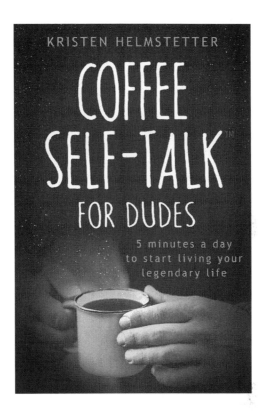

Coffee Self-Talk for Dudes:
5 Minutes a Day to Start Living Your Legendary Life

This is a special edition of *Coffee Self-Talk* that has been edited to be more oriented toward men in the language, examples, and scripts. It is 95% identical to the original Coffee Self-Talk book.

Made in the USA
Coppell, TX
17 September 2023

21688463R00081